Ask an Animal

This edition published in 2011 by
CHARTWELL BOOKS, INC.
a division of BOOK SALES, INC.
276 Fifth Avenue Suite 206
New York, New York 10001
USA

Conceived, edited, and designed by
Marshall Editions
The Old Brewery
6 Blundell Street
London N7 9BH, UK

ISBN-13: 978-0-7858-2899-0

Publisher: James Ashton-Tyler
Creative Director: Linda Cole
Editorial Director: Sorrel Wood
Project Editor: Elise See Tai
Editorial Project Manager: Emily Collins
Design: Ali Scrivens
Production: Nikki Ingram
Picture research: Clare Newman

Originated in Hong Kong by Modern Age
Printed and bound in Dongguan, China, by Toppan Leefung

10 9 8 7 6 5 4 3 2 1

Ask an Animal

Miranda Smith

CHARTWELL
BOOKS, INC.

Contents

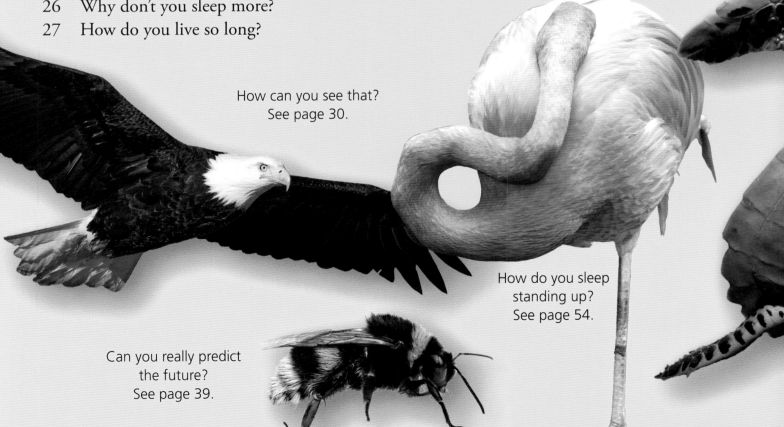

How can you see that?
See page 30.

How do you sleep
standing up?
See page 54.

Can you really predict
the future?
See page 39.

40 How Can You Live Like That?
Animals and extreme living

56 How Can You Do That?
Animals and super powers

Do you ever get lost? See page 24.

How do you make yourself invisible? See page 58.

How do you sing? See page 11.

Why Ask An Animal?

There are an amazing 10 million different kinds of animals in the world, from tiny insects, such as the leafcutter ant and wolf spider, to large **mammals**, like elephants and whales. And every one of these animals has developed special skills that help them survive in the wild. Some animals walk upside-down, while others fly backward. There are even some that sleep standing up or walk on water! In this book, find out exactly how they do these things—this is your opportunity to ask an animal all the questions you want them to answer.

How Do You Do That?

Animals and physical feats

Change color, like a chameleon. See page 17.

Grow new body parts, like a starfish. See page 16.

Balance on one leg,
like a flamingo.
See page 22.

Eat poo, like a dung beetle.
See page 15.

Walk upside-down, like a gecko.
See page 10.

How do you walk upside-down?

Some animals can run up a wall or walk upside-down on a ceiling. Several species of lizards and insects use their specially designed feet to do this. Some use their claws to cling to a surface while others make their own glue to help them stick!

Gecko

This lizard can run up any wall or across a ceiling when it chases an insect to eat. It can do this because its toes are covered with millions of **microscopic** hairs called setae (SEE-ti). These hairs help the gecko cling to smooth surfaces, even glass.

I also have toes that bend in the opposite direction from your fingers and toes. This means that I can easily peel my toes off the surfaces that I walk on.

Who else can walk upside-down?

Spider

A spider has claws that it uses to cling to rough surfaces. On each of the spider's feet are hairlike tufts. These tufts allow the spider to hold on to smooth surfaces. Spiders have eight feet, and each of them has an incredible 78,000 tiny hairs on it.

Fly

On a fly's foot are two footpads. The tiny hairs on these footpads produce sugars and oils. These mix to make a gluelike substance that helps the feet stick to smooth surfaces. Flies also have small claws to help them lever their feet off the surface when they want to move.

How do you sing?

Many different animals sing. Some of them, such as the whale, even sing while underwater! Like us, birds have vocal cords, but other animals, like frogs, have vocal sacs to help them make calls to their mates.

Common Yellowthroat

A bird's vocal cord, or **syrinx** (sih-rin-ks), is simpler than our vocal cords. The vocal cord is at the bottom of a bird's windpipe, much closer to its lungs. This means that birds can sing two different notes at the same time. Some birds are born with an instant ability to sing. Others learn to sing and copy their parent's calls and songs.

> I have a very beautiful and complicated song. I sing a particular song to attract a mate. She can hear me sing from a long way off. I also sing to keep other males out of my territory.

How did we sing?

In medieval times, musicians called troubadours (TROO-ba-dors) worked in towns and courts all over Europe. They composed and sang songs. They also acted out the stories that they sang.

Who else can sing?

Bullfrog

Male bullfrogs croak to show that they are healthy and strong. They make a deep call with the vocal sac under their throats. They croak to attract female bullfrogs. They also croak to warn other males to stay away from their **territory**.

Grasshopper

Male grasshoppers "sing" during the day to attract a mate. A row of bumps on the inside of the hind legs rub against a ridge on the wings. This causes a vibration and a chirping sound. Each different kind of grasshopper has a different song.

Who is the fastest?

There are some speedy animals in the animal kingdom and even the fastest human on Earth cannot move as fast as some of them. The animals on these two pages are some of the fastest, but the peregrine falcon is the quickest animal of all, as well as the fastest bird. On land, the cheetah has the record, while at sea, a sailfish would certainly win any race.

> I always stalk my prey first before chasing it. I can run very fast, but I can only do so for a short time. If I don't catch my prey in less than a minute, I have to give up.

Cheetah

This cat is very quick on land, sometimes traveling 75 mph (120 kph). It reaches speeds of 64 mph (102 kph) in only three seconds. Cheetahs run this fast when they are chasing their **prey**.

Who else is fast?

Ostrich

These big birds are excellent runners. Although they are too heavy to fly, they move very quickly on land. Ostriches travel at up to 45 mph (70 kph) for as long as 30 minutes at a time. They run on their two-toed feet.

Hare

The hares' long legs help them hop across fields very quickly. Their furry feet have hair on the soles that give them extra grip as they move. Hares spend all of their lives above ground. They can reach a speed of 35 mph (56 kph) when they are running away from danger.

Wildebeest

The wildebeest, or gnu, has to run fast to get away from big cats such as lions and cheetahs. Wildebeests can reach 40 mph (64 kph) or more as they run across the plains (areas with few trees) of Africa. Their long legs give them a long stride and they have two toes on each foot.

What can we do?

At the Olympic Games in 2008, a Jamaican sprinter named Usain Bolt became the fastest man in the world. He ran 656 ft. (200 m) in only 19.30 seconds. He has since broken his own record.

I am called a "wildebeest," which means "wild beast" in Dutch. I like to travel in big herds with other wildebeests. We need to run to stay safe from **predators**.

Peregrine falcon

The world's fastest bird, the peregrine falcon, dives at more than 100 mph (160 kph). This falcon catches its favorite prey, a pigeon, by knocking the bird from the air and following the prey to the ground. The peregrine's slim body, long, narrow tail, and pointed wings help it fly very fast.

Who is the strongest?

Size does not always matter when it comes to strength. Some of the smallest animals on Earth can carry incredibly heavy loads in comparison to their own body weight. The dung beetle is the record holder in this category. It is able to pull about 1,140 times its body weight—this is something we could only dream about!

Rhinoceros beetle

These are among the largest of all the beetles, but they are only about 2 in. (6 cm) long. The males have forked horns that they use to fight other males. They also use their horns as digging tools to help bury themselves if they are in danger. Rhinoceros beetles are very strong. They can lift up to 850 times their own weight!

I have a body that is covered by an external skeleton, called an exoskeleton. This protects me when I fight. I sometimes scare away animals with loud squeaks.

Who else is strong?

Gorilla

An adult male gorilla is about ten times more powerful than an adult human. It weighs up to 660 lbs. (300 kg), twice the weight of a female gorilla. It has large muscles in its arms that it uses for gathering plant food and to defend itself.

Leafcutter ant

These tiny insects slice off leaves up to 50 times their own body weight. They lift the leaves in their strong jaws and carry them back to the nest.

How can you eat that?

Some animals eat poo, others drink blood, and owls eat whole mice! This may sound disgusting to us, but their bodies are designed to be able to digest these strange things—and they need to eat them to survive.

Barn owl

This bird loves to eat mice. It does not have teeth, so it cannot chew. It swallows the whole mouse in chunks—bones, tail, and all. It then digests the parts that its body needs. Afterward, it brings up, or regurgitates (ree–GUR-jeh-tates), all the material that it cannot digest, such as feathers and fur, in the form of a pellet (below right).

> I am a hunter. I like to look for my prey at dusk as I swoop over the countryside. I have excellent vision and very sharp **talons** to grasp and kill small animals.

What can you do?

People all over the world eat and enjoy some very strange things. For example, there are recipes for jellied moose nose, slug fritters, scorpions dipped in chocolate, and bird's nest soup. What is your favorite?

Who else can eat strange things?

Vampire bat

These bats only eat blood. They have sharp teeth to cut into the skin of a bird, horse, or cow. Their **saliva** contains a special substance that stops their **prey's** blood from clotting. This means that the bat can lap up the blood more easily.

Dung beetle

As their name suggests, dung beetles eat animal poo. They shape it into balls and roll it away to bury it as food for their young. Farmers like dung beetles because they help fertilize the soil.

Why do you grow new body parts?

Some animals can grow new arms or legs. This handy trick helps the animals survive an attack and live longer. For these animals, this means that an attack from a **predator** is not always the end.

Starfish

When a starfish is attacked by a hungry fish, it often loses one or more of its arms. If this happens, it immediately starts to grow its missing limb. Sometimes, the chopped off limb develops into a completely new starfish.

What can you do?

Although we cannot grow whole arms, we can regrow fingernails and hair. We are also good at growing new skin when it is damaged. And we grow a whole new set of teeth when we lose our baby teeth.

I am quite slow at growing back any of my arms. It takes about a year for an arm to grow to its original size. I have only five arms, but some other starfish have as many as 50!

Who else can grow new body parts?

Earthworm

If you look closely at a worm, you will see that it has lots of rings on its body. A worm only needs the first 35 parts of its body because this is where its important organs are. If the tail part gets damaged, it can regrow. In some cases, if the first five segments at the head end get cut off, they too will grow to complete the body again.

Salamander

Regrowing body parts is key to the salamander's survival. If a bird attacks its tail, the salamander will simply shed its tail. The tail twitches on the ground and distracts the bird.

Why do you change color?

Some animals alter their appearance by changing the color of their skin or fur. There are many reasons for doing this. The animal may need to hide from a predator, or communicate with another member of its species, or perhaps even attract a mate. Some animals change color quickly, others take more time.

I change color when I am threatened! Light, temperature, mood, and health all play an important part in the color that I turn.

Can you?

Our skin color changes, too. People who have fair skin will slowly turn brown, or even red if they spend too long in the sun! Watch out or you will burn.

Chameleon

This lizard is nature's expert at changing color! When the chameleon is cold or angry, it turns a darker color by expanding the cells in its skin—the cells become larger. But when it wants to communicate with another member of its species, it **contracts** the cells—the cells become smaller. This causes many different colors to appear.

Who else can change color?

Cuttlefish

This fish is the chameleon of the seas. It creates many different colors and patterns to match different backgrounds when trying to escape from a predator, or communicate with other fish.

Arctic fox

This **mammal** changes color to match the seasons. In the short Arctic summer, its fur is brownish-gray. In the winter, its fur turns completely white to match the snowy landscape. During spring, it sheds the white coat and grows brown fur again.

What is special about your food?

Some animals can only eat one type of food and unlike us, they don't get bored! Some creatures only feed on plants—their bodies are designed for eating and digesting plant life and their bodies need the **nutrients** in order to survive.

> I am a **herbivore**, which means I only eat plants. Some other rhinos eat leaves and fruit. I use my top lip like a finger to pull food into my mouth.

Rhino

Rhinoceroses are very large and heavy plant-eaters. They have thick, tough skin that is like armor and nose horns that they use for defense. They have to eat a lot to get the nutrients that they need, so they graze in family groups all evening, through the night, and in the early morning.

Who else has special food?

Koala

The koala spends almost all its life in eucalyptus trees, and its only food is eucalyptus leaves (right). Each day, it eats about 1 lb. (500 g) of leaves. When it is not eating, it sleeps perched in the branches of a tree. Koalas are **marsupials**, **mammals** that raise their young inside a pouch.

How can you eat all that?

Some of the smallest animals can eat amazing amounts of food. Aardvarks have snouts to gobble their food up, while hamsters and shrews store it in their cheeks for later.

Pygmy shrew

A fully grown pygmy shrew is only about a quarter of the size of a house mouse. This tiny shrew has to eat food all the time. It needs to do so because very small bodies are difficult to keep warm. If it does not get enough fuel in the form of food, it runs out of energy and dies.

I need to eat my own weight in food every day! I like to eat spiders, worms, snails, and woodlice. I find my prey by smell and touch, and then give it a poisonous bite!

Who else can eat a lot?

Anaconda

Anacondas are the largest snakes in the world. They kill their large **prey** by coiling their bodies around their victims and squeezing. Then they unhinge their jaws and swallow the prey whole. They like to eat wild pigs, fish, deer, birds, turtles, caimans, and even jaguars.

Aardvark

These animals have an amazing appetite. They have large claws that they use to break into termite mounds and anthills. Then, they use their long, sticky tongues to sweep the insects into their tubelike snouts. They suck up to 50,000 insects at a time and swallow them whole.

19

How do you deal with bullies?

It is important to learn how to protect ourselves and animals are just the same. Animals have all sorts of tricks to frighten off others that are much bigger than themselves. Some defend themselves with weapons or even poison, while others are smart at hiding.

> I am very good at scaring away other fish! I expand, or increase, to more than twice my normal size, and if a predator isn't scared, my pointy **spines** will do the trick!

Puffer fish

A puffer fish swims very slowly, so if it is attacked, it cannot speed away. However, its name describes exactly what it does! It has a clever form of defense—the puffer fish gulps water, filling its very elastic stomach. It then blows itself up so that **predators**, such as a crab, cannot hold on to it.

Who else defends themselves?

Horned lizard

This lizard has a unique way of dealing with bullies. It squirts blood out of the corner of its eyes! It can hit a target over a distance of 5 ft. (1.5 m).

This action confuses a predator, and the blood tastes horrible.

Octopus

When threatened, an octopus may change color to make it seem as if it has disappeared. Or it may flee, hidden by an inky cloud that it releases into the water. It can also shoot a jet of water through its body to give it a burst of speed.

Why do you carry your babies?

Baby animals often need to be carried to protect them from danger. Some animals, such as kangaroos, carry their young in pouches, but there are lots of other ways that animal babies can be transported.

I lay up to 80 eggs at a time, so I have a lot of work to do carrying my babies to the water. I have to be very careful not to hurt them with my big, sharp teeth.

Crocodile

A female Nile crocodile lays eggs in sandy ground high on the riverbank. When the babies hatch, their mother might lead them to the water. Most often, though, she carries them to the water in her mouth.

Who else carries their young?

Lioness

Lionesses live together in a group called a **pride** and look after each other's cubs. When the lion cubs are small, they cannot run very fast. If necessary, like other big cats, a lioness will carry a cub to safety by the scruff of its neck.

Wolf spider

This spider has a special way of looking after its young. Immediately after the **spiderlings** (young spiders) hatch from their egg sac, they climb up their mother's legs. They crowd onto her back and stay there until they are big enough to survive on their own.

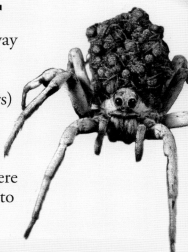

How do you balance so well?

Some animals are really good at standing on one leg and can do so for a long time. Others are experts at balancing, or standing upright on slippery slopes. Strong leg muscles help them balance for longer than we can.

Flamingo

This bird often stands on one leg, tucking the other leg up against its body. It does not seem to prefer standing on one leg rather than the other. Why flamingos do this has been a bit of a mystery that scientists have only solved recently (see speech bubble).

I like to take a nap with my head tucked under my wing. I always do this standing on one leg because it means that I can keep more heat in my body.

What do we do?

We need to have good balance just to stay upright. Some acrobats are very good at balancing. They can walk along a thin bar as easily as they walk along the ground.

Who else can balance?

Chamois goat

These mountain goats live on steep hillsides. They are very sure-footed animals that can run easily across slippery rocks. They are also good jumpers and can leap up in the air as high as 6½ ft. (2 m) to go from ledge to ledge.

Stick bug

These insects are also called walking sticks. They live in trees and bushes, balanced on the twigs that they look like. They feed mostly on leaves and move quickly from one branch to another.

What do you do with all those spines?

Some animals have a different kind of hair—these are **spines**. Spines are sharp and pointy and are used for protection. Sometimes they lie flat and other times they stand upright so that they can injure or scare away **predators**.

Porcupine

A porcupine has a coat of sharp spines known as quills that are up to 14 in. (35 cm) long. They use these spines to defend themselves from predators. The quills stick into the skin of the attacker and they are very painful.

> I am really good at getting rid of attackers. If I am threatened, I raise my quills and rattle my tail before charging backward.

Who else has spines?

Hedgehog

When a hedgehog finds itself in danger, it does not need to run away. Its back is covered with about 6,000 sharp spines. It rolls itself into a ball and makes its spines stand on end. This makes it very hard for a predator to pick it up or bite it.

Sea urchin

A sea urchin has a round, spine-covered body. Some sea urchins have sharp spines that snap off in the body of a predator. Others use their spines to jam themselves into rocky crevices so that they cannot be eaten.

Do you ever get lost?

Animals don't have satellite navigation to help them find their way around, so how do they know where to go? Some animals, such as penguins, follow coastlines, while salmon use their sense of smell to find the exact stream in which they were born.

Birds use the Sun, Moon, and stars to **navigate**. Some animals **migrate**—they move from one place to another according to the time of year and know exactly where to go.

Turtles

Some sea turtles migrate long distances from their feeding grounds to beaches where they lay their eggs. Scientists think that turtles navigate by a mixture of the Earth's magnetic field, the taste of the water, and memory.

I follow my own map of the Earth's oceans. I travel to my birth place to lay my eggs. I know the ocean really well, so I don't need to worry about getting lost.

Who else can find their way home?

Penguin

Each year, Adelie penguins travel in large groups 3,400 mi. (5,500 km) around the edge of Antarctica to their winter feeding grounds. Then they travel back again to breed. Their nesting colonies (groups) are vast, containing more than one million birds.

Salmon

These fish have an incredible memory and a great sense of smell. This enables them to travel thousands of miles (km) from the sea to the stream where they were born. Salmon can do this because they survive in both salt and freshwater. Once they swim upriver, they lay their eggs, then swim back to sea.

Wildebeest

Africa is so hot and dry that wildebeests have to travel far to find fresh plants to feed on. Large herds of wildebeests migrate hundreds of miles (km). They follow the direction of the rain and the smell of the wildebeests in front of them, so they never lose their way.

What can you do?

Unlike these animals, we cannot smell our way home or rely on feeling the pull of the Earth. This is why we need to use maps to plan our route and find our way.

What did we do?

In prehistoric times, people used nature to help them navigate. They learned that the Sun rises in the east and sets in the west. They used stars to help find their way north.

I follow the rain! I can sense thunderstorms that are up to 30 mi. (48 km) away. I follow the rains across Africa. I remember the direction of the rain, so I never get lost!

Arctic tern

This extraordinary bird travels farther than any other animal on Earth—an amazing 43,000 mi. (70,000 km). Every year, these birds breed in the Arctic, then travel to Antarctica, where they spend the winter. In spring, they travel all the way back again.

Why don't you sleep more?

All animals have to sleep, either to give their brains or their bodies a rest. However, there are some animals that appear to need very little sleep. They may sleep less to avoid attack from **predators** or may not have time to sleep longer because of travel or the way they live.

Giraffe

Adult giraffes do not need very much sleep. They only sleep properly for about 20 minutes to 2 hours a day. They go into a deep sleep for about 20 minutes, and the rest of their sleep is split into a series of shorter naps.

I always sleep standing up. I like to rest my head on my hindquarters when I go to sleep. But I need to be on my feet in case I need to run away from a predator.

Who else has so little sleep?

Migrating birds

Many birds, such as these pelicans, travel hundreds of miles (km) to find warmer weather. Some birds travel during the day. Others, such as owls, travel at night. While they are traveling, there is not much time for sleep, so the birds take hundreds of naps that only last a few seconds.

Dolphin

A dolphin sleeps in a very interesting way. It cannot go into a deep sleep because it has to be conscious in order to reach the surface regularly to breathe. So half of the dolphin's brain naps, while the other half is alert and ready for action.

How do you live so long?

There are some animals that live for a very long time—longer than we could ever survive. Ocean quahogs, a type of clam, can live for more than 400 years, tuatara lizards live between 100 and 200 years, and the oldest known bowhead whale was 211 years old.

I think I am the most beautiful of the macaws, as well as the most intelligent. I like to fly over the rain forest to look for nuts and seeds to eat.

What do we do?

Some people live for a very long time indeed. The record holder is a Frenchwoman, Jeanne Calment, who lived to the ripe old age of 122 years and 164 days.

Blue-and-yellow macaw

These colorful South American birds can live up to 60 years. They do not breed until they are about three or four years old, but probably stay with the same mate for life. They nest high above the ground in holes in large, dead trees.

Who else lives for a long time?

Giant tortoise

These rare **reptiles** are thought to be the longest-living vertebrates (animals with backbones) on Earth. In 2006, a giant tortoise named Adwaita died. After dating the shell, it was thought that the tortoise was about 255 years old.

Carp

These fish are known as koi in Japan. Some species live for more than 200 years. The oldest known was a pet koi named Hanako. It outlived several owners and died at the age of 226 on July 7, 1977.

How Do You Know That?

Animals and super senses

See in the dark, like a bat. See page 31.

Hear without earflaps, like a fish. See page 33.

Taste with your tentacles, like an octopus. See page 35.

Smell with your tongue, like a snake.
See page 36.

Predict the future, like an elephant.
See page 39.

How can you see that?

Some animals have very sharp eyesight. We would need binoculars to see distances as far as an eagle, hawk, or owl can see. And we cannot see behind us like some animals can, such as the mantis shrimp. These animals need their super sight in order to survive in the wild.

My eyes are on the side of my skull. They can see outward and forward, and this overlapping vision helps me to work out distances exactly. I need to be able to do that to catch fish!

What can you do?

We can use different machines to help us see things. Binoculars and telescopes bring distant objects closer. Microscopes show us tiny things that we cannot see otherwise.

Eagle

All eagles have excellent eyesight. The bald eagle can spot a fish near the surface of the water from several hundred feet (m) above it. This bird's eye is almost as large as your eye, but its eyesight is at least four times sharper.

Who else can see well?

Mantis shrimp

The mantis shrimp has its eyes mounted on mobile stalks. It has the most complex eyes of any animal and can see objects with three different parts of the eye. One part is specialized for color vision.

Flounder

A flounder is a flatfish that has both eyes on the same side of its flat body. This allows the fish to lie on the ocean floor with both eyes looking upward. These fish find their food by sight rather than smell or feel, like most others do.

How do you see in the dark?

Night hunters, such as bats and cats, can see much better when it is dark because they have special abilities that help them hunt for **prey** when there is little light.

> I can tell how big an insect is when I squeak. If one of the moths I like to eat is small, it will have a weaker echo. I can also tell whether the moth is flying toward me because the pitch of the echo will be higher than my squeak.

Bat

A bat has a real advantage in the dark. It uses a special navigation system called echolocation to find its way around. It makes squeaking noises that bounce back, or echo, off any objects that are in its way. Some bats send out the sound from their mouths, while others send it out through their noses.

Who else can see in the dark?

Rattlesnake

A rattlesnake can see heat. It has special heat pits near its eyes that let it "see" infrared images. These allow the rattlesnake to detect its prey by the creature's body heat. Rattlesnakes track down prey, such as a small **mammal**, from up to 30 ft. (9 m) away.

Wildcat

Cats have great night vision. They see clearly with only a sixth of the light that we need. Their pupils widen until they become large circles. This lets in more light. Then a mirrorlike membrane in the back of the eye gives the cat a second chance of seeing.

Why do you have so many eyes?

Animal eyes can look different and can behave differently from ours. Some animals have more than two eyes to help them make their way around. Many insects and crustaceans have only two eyes, but their eyes are more complex.

> I have really clever eyes. Each of the parts, or facets, faces in a slightly different direction. This means that I can see anything nearby and react really quickly!

Fly

A fly has compound eyes. These are made up of hundreds of light-sensitive parts that are connected by nerves to its brain. These eyes allow the fly to see in most directions at once so it can spot any changes in what it is looking at much more quickly than we can with our eyes.

What do we do?

In our brain, we "see" the light information sent to it from our eyes. The retina at the back of the eye collects light signals and sends them as electrical signals to the brain.

Who else has a lot of eyes?

Scallop

It is easy to see the bright blue eyes of a scallop. There are 50 to 100 of them in rows just along the edge of its shell. If any of the eyes are lost or injured, the mollusk will simply regrow them.

Box jellyfish

A box jellyfish has 24 eyes. They are on cuplike structures that hang from its body. As it swims, some of the eyes help the jellyfish to dart around obstacles. Some of them detect the light levels, and some of them see the color and size of objects.

How can you hear without ears?

Some animals don't have ear openings like ours. Instead, they "hear" sounds in a different way. Some animals can pick up noise through hairs or through their bodies and bones!

I can sense pressure changes in the water with my body. I have a special row of sensors called the lateral line system. This helps me feel nearby fish moving in the water.

Fish

A fish does not have holes for ears or protective earflaps like we do. Its ears are inside its skull. Sound waves go right through the fish's body to its bones and travel up to the skull. Here, ear stones—the equivalent to our inner ear bones—send a message to the brain.

What do we do?

Sound is made up of energy waves. These waves travel in the air toward us. We have ear canals, openings, that allow the sound waves into our ears. The ear canal channels the vibrations made by the waves down to the ear drum and inner ear.

Who else can hear without ears?

Spider

A spider, such as this tarantula, does not have ears. Instead, there are very tiny hairs on its legs. When a noise is made, the hairs pick up pressure waves in the air. That is why you often see a spider stretching out its front legs.

Cricket

The ears of a cricket are not in a place you would expect! In fact, the cricket's ears are just below the knees of its front legs. By turning around, a cricket can tell what direction a sound is coming from.

How do you taste things?

Many animals use taste to find foods they like. Some have a different way of tasting flavors than we do. Rabbits, for example, have many more taste buds than humans. Others have sensors in a completely different place to where you would expect. Butterflies have sensors in their feet!

> I nibble all day and chew 120 times a minute. I eat dandelion leaves, herbs, and grasses. I can eat all kinds of plants, even ones that other animals can't digest.

Rabbit

A rabbit has about 17,000 taste buds in its mouth—we only have about 10,000. So a rabbit is much more sensitive to differences in the taste of its food. Rabbits are **herbivores** that feed by grazing on grass and leafy plants. They also eat their own droppings in order to extract, or take in, all the **nutrients** from the plants that they possibly can.

How do other animals taste food?

Pig

A pig's tongue has three or four times as many taste buds as we have. Like its ancestor, the wild boar, a pig eats almost any kind of food, including plants, meat, and birds' eggs.

Earthworm

An earthworm has a special taste organ just behind its mouth. Its whole body is also covered in tiny sense organs called chemoreceptors (KEE-MO-reh-sep-ters) that can detect chemicals in the soil. These help it to find food.

Butterfly

Some animals do not have taste sensors in their mouths. When a butterfly lands on a flower, it is looking for nectar on which to feed. The insect uses the taste sensors in its feet to guide it to the nectar, which it sucks up with its long proboscis (pro-BOH-suhs), or mouthpart.

What do we do?

We have lots of taste buds on our tongue. The food and drink that we put in our mouth combines with our **saliva** to send information to the taste buds. Special cells called papillae (pah-PIL-EE) in the taste buds detect the different tastes.

> I can taste things with my feet. I can tell that I would like to eat something simply by walking on it. I only feed on liquids such as sweet nectar from flowers and water from the damp places that I visit.

Octopus

The octopus tastes with the suckers on its **tentacles**. This means that it does not have to leave the safety of the crevice it is living in to get food. It can simply stretch out its tentacles and pull in a tasty fish.

Where is your nose?

Most animals have a great sense of smell. It helps some animals to find food and others to avoid becoming a meal for a **predator**, but they don't always use their nose to smell. Snakes use their tongues!

Python

When a snake flicks out its tongue, it is using it to smell! The tongue is forked—it is split into two points. When the tongue flicks back, the two points go to two openings on the roof of its mouth leading to a sensitive spot called a Jacobson's organ. This organ checks out the smells and sends a message to the snake's brain.

I live in a world of smells. To find out what is around the corner, I shoot out my tongue and flick it up and down to pick up scents from the air and ground.

What can we do?

How good is your sense of smell? We recognize thousands of smells, but our smelling ability is probably at its best from the age of 8 until about 30.

How do others smell?

Albatross

The albatross, like many other seabirds, has a very well-developed sense of smell. It spends its time flying above the ocean looking for fish. Its extra-large nose helps it spot food, even in the dark.

Shark

You have to be very careful around sharks. A large part of their brain is devoted to smell. They may not be able to see that far in murky seawater but they have no trouble smelling a tiny drop of blood up to 0.6 mi. (1 km) away.

How can you smell that?

Most vertebrate animals have a sense of smell that is far superior to ours. These animals have more nerve cells in their noses. This gives them an advantage when they are looking for food or a mate, or when they are trying to avoid danger.

> I lift my head up to catch any smells drifting toward me. I really like the smell of ripe fruit, buds, berries, and nuts.

Black bear

The part of a bear's brain devoted to smell is five times larger than a human's. It has a large nose, and inside its nostrils are thousands of smell receptors that help it find food. It tears open old logs for worms and grubs and will gnaw its way into a tree to reach the honey in a beehive.

Who else can smell that?

Eel

These fish cannot see or hear well, but they rely on an acute sense of smell to locate their **prey**. Marine eels live in shallow coastal waters. They are **nocturnal**, hunting at night, and **ambush** fish that swim by.

Star-nosed mole

This furry **mammal** has very poor eyesight because it lives underground. But its sense of smell is highly developed. It sniffs and feels prey with the 22 **tentacles** around its nose. The tentacles never stop wriggling and moving!

Why do you need whiskers?

Some animals use the whiskers on their face to help them detect obstacles or find **prey**. Some whiskers are very long and help the animal feel their way. Other animals' whiskers have taste buds and help them sense food.

Leopard

Most big cats have at least 24 long whiskers, 12 on each side of their nose. The whiskers are more than twice as thick as ordinary hairs, and their roots are set very deep in their skin. They have lots of nerve endings that send information to the brain.

> I use my whiskers to help me feel my way around. When I am angry, I pull my whiskers back, but when I am happy, I am more relaxed and so my whiskers go forward.

Who else needs whiskers?

Catfish

This fish has whiskerlike organs called **barbels** (BAR-buhls) that hang around its mouth. The barbels are covered with taste buds that help catfish find prey in dark water.

Sea lion

Sea lions (right) and seals are **mammals** that spend most of their lives in the water. They have long whiskers that they use to help them feel their way in the water. The whiskers sense the vibration of their prey.

Can you really predict the future?

Many animals are sensitive to tiny temperature changes and this affects their behavior, sometimes making them run away or hide. In this way, they sometimes know something is wrong before others do.

Elephant

Scientists think that animals such as elephants use their five senses more efficiently than we do. They are more sensitive to changes in the atmosphere, and this helps them. For example, in Thailand in 2004, elephants tried to reach high ground to escape a tsunami (SOO-nah-MEE), a giant wave, before people knew about the danger.

I can tell when something dangerous is happening because I feel shock waves and rumblings in the ground through my feet. These scare me and make me run away as fast as I can.

Who else can predict the future?

Dog

Dogs seem to be able to sense things that people cannot. They often bark or whine just before an earthquake. It is possible that they act like this because they feel the earth vibrate before we do.

Bumblebee

In the summer, you can predict the weather by watching the bees. If they are particularly busy collecting pollen, then good weather is coming. If there are not many around, it is probably going to rain.

How Can You Live Like That?

Animals and extreme living

Hibernate all winter, like a tortoise. See page 50.

Manage without water, like a camel. See page 49.

Take over a shell, like a hermit crab.
See page 52.

Sleep standing up, like a giraffe.
See page 55.

Survive the cold, like a polar bear.
See page 44.

How do you live so deep in the sea?

Deep down in the dark world of the ocean depths, there are some extraordinary animals. They have developed ways of surviving despite the fact that there is no light and the temperature is near freezing.

I can live in very cold water but also where it is warmer. Sometimes down here there are millions of us looking for microbes on the rocks and in the water.

Shrimp

Deep-sea shrimp live in the cold parts of the Atlantic and Pacific ocean. They are usually found in soft mud on the seafloor. Some species swim up from below 1,500 ft. (450 m) every night in the surface waters. They feed on the **microscopic** plants, called **plankton** (PLANK-tan), that float.

What else lives deep in the sea?

Spiky oreo

Adult spiky oreo fish swim around in the sea at depths of up to 4,250 ft. (1,300 m), feeding on fish, crustaceans, and squid. Their eggs float near the surface and the **larvae** also swim in the surface.

Anglerfish

A piece of the anglerfish's **spine**, called a lure, sticks out from its head. The end of the spine shines because of a light-producing organ called a **photophore** (FO-TOE-for). The anglerfish uses this spine to tempt **prey** to get close enough for its tooth-filled mouth to grab the creature. Its teeth are angled inward, and this stops the prey from escaping.

What can we do?

We cannot stay underwater for long and we cannot dive as deep as the animals on these pages. To explore the ocean depths, we need to use a deep sea submarine.

Sperm whale

Like all whales, this whale has lungs and must come to the surface to breathe. But a sperm whale can dive deeper than any other **mammal**. It is thought that sperm whales can reach depths of 3,000 ft. (1,000 m) and stay underwater for two hours at a time.

Gulper eel

This umbrella-mouth gulper eel lives in the deep ocean. Its enormous mouth is larger than its body. The end of the long, whiplike tail has a light-producing organ that glows pink and red. The eel uses this like a fishing line to attract fish. When prey gets close enough, the eel lunges and snaps it up.

How do you survive the cold?

Some animals are experts at keeping warm in freezing temperatures. Some, such as penguins, have feathers to keep out the cold. Others, like polar bears and seals, have lots of fur, as well as extra-thick layers of fat on their bodies that stop their body heat from escaping too fast.

Polar bears

The polar bear lives in one of the coldest places on Earth—the Arctic. Their thick, oily fur is waterproof and protects them when they hunt ringed seals in the icy waters. In winter, they dig snow dens to take shelter away from the freezing wind and snowstorms.

I eat as much food as I can. It helps me build up fat, and this fat keeps me warm during the cold winter. My thick fur helps, too.

Who else can survive the cold?

Ice fish

Ice fish live in very deep, very cold water. Their large hearts and special blood mean that they can survive in temperatures that would freeze other fish.

Penguins

In winter, the Emperor penguin keeps its egg warm. It huddles close to other penguins and puts the egg on its feet, covered by its feathers, until the egg hatches. The chick huddles with other chicks.

How do you stay so still?

Some animals, such as deer, are very good at staying still in order to protect themselves. Other animals stay motionless as a hunting strategy in order to **ambush** unsuspecting **prey** as soon as they come within range of attack!

I stay hidden in the grass for the first week of my life because I am not strong enough to walk around. I have to stay still so that others cannot see me.

Red deer fawn

If a young deer, or fawn, stays very still, it will not be seen by a **predator**. Their scent glands have not developed, so predators cannot smell them. Fawns also have reddish-brown and spotted coats that help **camouflage** (ka-MOO-flahj) (hide) them. The spots disappear when the fawn is three to four months old.

Who else can stay still?

Trapdoor spider

This spider digs a burrow in the ground and makes a trapdoor out of soil, vegetation, and its silk. It stays very still in the burrow until something hits the trip lines that it has left around the trapdoor. Then, the spider leaps out and grabs its prey.

Rabbit

If there is a threat, a rabbit may thump its foot to warn other rabbits. If a predator gets too close, the rabbit can bite, kick, or run to its hole. It can also stay absolutely still in the undergrowth until the danger passes.

How do you see in water?

There are animals that spend all or most of their lives in water. To see clearly in what are often very murky conditions, some of them have developed particular abilities. Many of these animals have special eyes.

What do we do?

We cannot see underwater clearly. This is because the angle that light bends is different when it travels between water and the eye than the angle it bends when it travels between air and the eye.

Penguin

Penguins are the expert swimmers in the cold southern seas. They hunt their **prey** of **krill**, squid, and fish in the dark waters. So how can they see these creatures in the dark? The transparent front part of a penguin's eye, the cornea (KOR-NEE-ah), is flat. This helps the eye see and focus sharply underwater.

I can dive underwater for up to 20 minutes before I need to come up to the surface for air. I "fly" through the water after my prey by flapping my wings.

Who else can see in and out of water?

Hippopotamus

A hippo spends lots of time in rivers, with only the top of its head showing. It has small ears, eyes, and nostrils. It can close its ears and nostrils so it can stay underwater for six minutes.

Four-eyed fish

This fish's eyes can see in air and water at the same time. They do not have four eyes. Instead, each of their two eyes is divided by flaps. This means there is one opening in the air and one in the water.

How do you stand the heat?

In some of the hottest places on Earth, there are some amazing animals living in incredible temperatures. These animals have developed ways of surviving— some only come out at night, others survive days without a drink.

I have thick, tough skin. This stops me from losing moisture. I don't waste energy chasing prey. I wait until it gets close enough and then strike with my deadly bite.

Rattlesnake

Many rattlesnakes live in desert regions. They shelter during the day and hunt when it is cooler at night. If they need to cross hot desert sands, they snake from side to side in a movement called sidewinding. This means that only a small part of their body is in contact with the sand at any one time.

Who else can stand the heat?

Giant tubeworms

These animals live at the bottom of the Pacific Ocean near "**black smokers**," where super-heated water from below Earth's crust comes through the ocean floor. The tubeworms feed on tiny bacteria.

Wild donkey

The large ears of this animal (also known as the wild ass) help keep it cool in the hot, rocky deserts where it lives. Its digestive system can cope with the tough plants. It can also go without water for several days, if necessary.

Why do you build homes like that?

Birds make nests to protect their eggs and chicks. Some insects, such as termites, ants, and wasps, live in large colonies like nests to protect their young.

If I can't attract a female with a nest, I'll start building another one until the right female comes along.

Weaver bird

The male weaver bird builds the most elaborate nest of any bird. He does it to attract a female with his building skills! Most species of weavers construct rounded nests, while others weave nests with long entrance tubes. They use any material that is available—grass, twigs, leaves, or stems of palm trees.

Who else builds strange homes?

Storks

These birds build some of the largest nests. Nests are usually made of sticks and lined with grasses, earth, rags, and paper. They can be used year after year.

Termites

There can be up to one million termites in a colony. Termites build giant nests up to 20 ft. (6 m) high. Each colony has a queen, and she alone lays eggs. The other termites find food and defend the nest.

How do you survive without water?

Animals can adapt to the most difficult conditions. Most desert animals are surprisingly good at managing with little or no water. Instead, they get what they need from the water they save and the food that they eat.

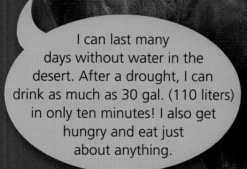

I can last many days without water in the desert. After a drought, I can drink as much as 30 gal. (110 liters) in only ten minutes! I also get hungry and eat just about anything.

Camel

Camels do not store water in their humps. They store fat there instead, and the hump acts as a food reserve when food is scarce. What they actually do to survive without water is drink a lot of water when they have the opportunity.

Who else can survive without water?

Oryx

This antelope gets most of its water from the plants it eats. It can go for weeks without a drink. Its kidneys help stop it from losing water, and it only sweats when its body temperature is more than 116°F (46°C).

Darkling beetle

When fog passes over the dry desert of Africa, some darklings stand on their heads. Moisture vapor changes into water on their bodies and rolls into their mouths. Other darklings dig to collect moisture/fog.

for so long?

Some animals sleep through the night, while some are **nocturnal** and sleep during the day. But some animals go to sleep for months or even years, through winters or droughts. They do this in order to survive.

What do we do?

We all need sleep. Our body needs a rest, and our brain needs the time to process all the information that it gathered during the day. The average person needs six to eight hours of sleep every day.

Tortoise

If a tortoise lives in a place where there are cold winters, it goes to sleep for several months. During this process, which is called **hibernation** (HI-bur-NAY-shun), its body temperature gets lower, its breathing is slower, and it uses very little energy. The tortoise's "sleep" is much deeper than human sleep, where loud noises might wake us up.

I have to eat lots of food during the warm weather—I like weeds, wild grasses, and flowers best. This builds up the stores of fat that my body needs while I am hibernating.

Who else sleeps for a long time?

Spadefoot toad

This toad hibernates underground in the winter, waking up with the warm weather and rain. When it gets hot, some spadefoots **estivate** (es-tih-VAYT)—go to sleep during the dry weather. They dig down 3 ft. (1 m) and encase, or cover, themselves in a watertight cocoon (protective covering) of skin. They are able to lose up to 48 percent of their body moisture.

> I hold on to the branches with my strong, curved claws. If I go to sleep, I am very safe hanging from a high branch. I wake up at night and look—very slowly—for the plants I like to eat. I munch on the leaves very slowly, too.

Sloth

The sloth spends most of its life hanging upside down in trees. During the day, it stays completely still, and when it does move, it moves very slowly. Despite the fact that people think sloths sleep a lot, they probably only doze for the same number of hours as we do.

Brown bear

When a bear hibernates, its sleep is much less deep than many other animals. Its temperature does not get much lower than normal and it can wake up quickly. Bear cubs are born in the bear's den during the winter months. The mother is awake enough to look after them, although she also sleeps a lot.

Dormouse

This **rodent** is nocturnal. It is awake at night, and during the day it sleeps in a nest several feet off the ground, often in a hollow tree branch. It builds its nest from bark that it weaves into a ball. It hibernates for six months in the winter.

Why do you stay in someone else's home?

Some animals go and live in other animals' homes uninvited. The home may have been abandoned, or still house another animal. In the case of the cuckoo, the invasion is not a welcome one. This is a way of life for some animals, and they usually do it because there is no other choice for survival.

I fit very snugly into my adopted home. I can pull my whole body back into the shell if I need to. From time to time, as I grow, I look for bigger shells and change houses.

Hermit crab

The hermit crab is really good at recycling! It finds an empty shell, usually the shell of a sea snail, and backs into it. The shell protects its soft body, and its claws stop anything from getting in.

Who else borrows a house?

Goby

This fish (below left) has a good way of sharing a home. The burrowing shrimp (below right) digs its burrow in which they both live. The shrimp cannot see very well, so in return for sharing, the goby flicks the shrimp with its tail whenever there is danger.

Cuckoo

Some cuckoos lay their eggs in the nests of other birds. The cuckoo egg hatches earlier, and the cuckoo chick pushes the other eggs out of the nest. This ensures that it has the undivided attention of the nest owners, which feed it constantly.

How do you find your way around?

Some animals live deep underground or in dark water where there is no light, but they have no problem moving around. They usually have very poor eyesight, but instead use other senses to help them find their way and find food.

Naked mole rat

This burrowing **rodent** lives in colonies underground. It digs through the earth with its large front teeth, searching for roots and bulbs to eat. It has an almost hairless, wrinkled body. Because it lives in darkness, its eyes are tiny and can only just make out the difference between light and dark.

I live underground with my family and friends—up to 300 of them! I have sensitive hairs all over my body that help me to find my way.

Who else can find their way in the dark?

Texas blind salamander

This salamander lives in complete darkness in streams in underground caverns (large caves). It cannot see because it does not need to, but it has two small, black eyespots where its eyes would be. Instead of finding **prey** by sight, it hunts snails and shrimp by sensing tiny movements in the water.

Blindfish

These fish, sometimes called cavefish, live in underground streams, deep oceans, or muddy waters. Some are born with eyes, but they soon lose their sight. The fish has sense organs that help it feel its way around.

Why do you sleep standing up?

Some animals have a neat trick of being able to sleep on their feet. The ones that do this are mostly four-legged grazers who are digesting their food while standing. There are also other reasons for this unusual habit.

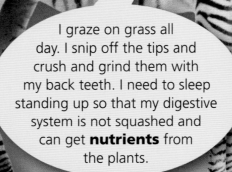

I graze on grass all day. I snip off the tips and crush and grind them with my back teeth. I need to sleep standing up so that my digestive system is not squashed and can get **nutrients** from the plants.

What do we do?

One of the reasons that we need to sleep is that we need to dream. Dreaming allows our brains to filter through the day's events, sort out new memories, and store information.

Zebra

It is an advantage for a zebra to be able to sleep standing up. It has great hearing and an excellent sense of smell. It can sense a **predator**, such as a big cat, approaching and be ready to run away quickly.

Who else sleeps standing up?

Horse

A horse is able to sleep both standing up and lying down. Horses do not sleep for long periods of time. Instead, they take standing rests regularly and occasionally lie down for a short, deep sleep.

Flamingo

This bird lives on salt flats, where the land is covered with salt. It can't sit down. Flamingos do not only sleep standing up, but even more amazingly, they do so on only one leg. When one side of their body is rested, they change legs.

Giraffe

A giraffe is one of the few animals in the world that is always on its feet. It only sleeps for short periods at a time, and always does this standing up. It is a large animal and would find it very difficult to scramble to its feet quickly if it was attacked while lying down.

I lock my legs in one place when I go to sleep. I also make sure my legs are in line with one another vertically. This means I don't have to use my muscles to keep them in place.

What did we do?

Astronauts in space, where there is no gravity, float around a spaceship as there is nothing to pull them down toward the ground. They go to sleep tied into special beds so they stay safe and don't float away.

Baboon

Guinea baboons sleep together in large troops high up in trees. Some of them sit on their heels for the night because this helps them stay alert to danger from predators, such as leopards.

How Can You Do That?

Animals and super powers

Ooze poison, like a poison dart frog.
See page 74.

Enjoy a good laugh, like a chimpanzee.
See page 72.

Hoot, like a gibbon.
See page 69.

Pretend to taste bad,
like a viceroy butterfly.
See page 70.

Scare with false eyes, like a spicebush caterpillar.
See page 67.

How do you make yourself invisible?

Some animals are very good at hiding. They can do this because their color or shape helps disguise them in their **environment**. So, while they might not be invisible, they are very hard to spot! This is useful when **predators** are around.

Crab spider

This spider is very difficult to see against the flowers that it visits. This particular species can change color in order to merge, or blend in, with its surroundings. It is yellow on this flower but can turn white or pale green to match flowers of other colors.

I catch my **prey** by **ambushing** them. I stay very still on the petals of the flower and wait. I have a poisonous bite that can kill a bee that is much larger than myself.

What do we do?

To **camouflage** ourselves, we wear clothing that helps us blend in with the landscape. Soldiers use snowsuits as camouflage in cold places and khaki-colored uniforms in forests or deserts.

Who else can make themselves invisible?

Cookiecutter shark

This deep-sea animal glows underneath its body from chin to tail. It does this as a form of camouflage. If prey is swimming underneath the shark, the glow looks like the sunlight or moonlight in the waters above. This helps the shark blend in so it can't be seen. The prey does not know that the shark is there until it is too late!

Leaf insect

It is very difficult for predators to catch a leaf insect. It usually looks so much like a leaf that if it stays still it cannot be seen. Even if it walks, the predator is still fooled because the leaf insect rocks back and forth, copying the movement of a leaf blowing in the wind.

I look just like the leaves on this guava tree. I am sometimes called a "walking leaf" for good reason! Being well camouflaged is very important for my protection, because I can't fly.

Cryptic frog

This **amphibian** has developed the color and shape that it needs to hide among the fallen leaves that cover the forest floor where it lives. Its head has hard angles that look like the edges of leaves and twigs, while its body color matches the fallen leaf shades of orange and brown.

Plaice

When a plaice is newly hatched, it lives near the surface. Then its left eye slowly moves across its head to its right side and it can lie flat on the seafloor. Its upper side changes color rapidly to suit the environment. It is impossible for predators to see the fish camouflaged in this way.

Can you fly backward?

There are birds and insects that have the ability to fly in any direction—

I am very good at hovering near my favorite plants so I can push my bill right inside a flower to get all the nectar. I can move in any direction and I sometimes even fly upside-down!

up, down, forward, backward. This gives some creatures, like hummingbirds, more control and allows them to travel or move as they want to.

Hummingbird

Hummingbirds can hover in midair and they are the only type of bird that can fly backward. A hummingbird beats its wings in a figure eight pattern. This means they have great control and can move in any direction. Some smaller species of hummingbirds beat their wings as quickly as 80 times a second.

Who else can fly backward?

Bumblebee

Bumblebees are more like a helicopter than an airplane. They have four flexible wings that flap and swivel. The movement of a bumblebee's wings is forward and backward, and it can fly up to 10 mph (16 kph).

Dragonfly

The dragonfly's wings work independently from each other. Their wings twist on the downstroke, which creates a miniature whirlwind. The whirlwind moves the air faster over the upper wing surface, reducing air pressure and increasing lift.

How do you move like that?

Animals do not wear shoes, but they have a variety of different ways to protect their bodies from the wet or heat. This sometimes means that they look a little funny when they move! Some animals have a special way of walking, others slither over hot sand, and some use limbs that you wouldn't expect them to.

I change color to keep cool. I am almost black every morning to help me absorb heat better. During the heat of the day, I turn gray to reflect light and stay cool.

Desert chameleon

This African lizard has a large, triangular head and a round body. It has developed a very smart way of walking across hot desert sands. It looks funny as it moves along using diagonally opposite limbs. Its ability to change color also helps keep it cool in the scorching desert heat.

Who else moves oddly?

Sidewinder

Many snakes sidewind, but the sidewinder is an expert at this movement. It throws itself sideways over the sand in a diagonal path. This uses less energy and less of its body touches the hot sand. These snakes also have a pair of horns over their eyes that work like sunglasses.

Mudskipper

This fish uses its pectoral (PEK-tor-ruhl) (front) fins to walk on land. It moves along in a series of skips. It can even climb up **mangrove** tree roots in the swamps. It can survive out of water because it breathes through both its gills and its skin.

How can you jump so high?

Many animals, such as frogs, dolphins, and kangaroos, jump or hop to move along, or when they are trying to escape from a **predator**. Some can leap incredible heights or across massive distances. They usually have incredibly strong and muscular legs.

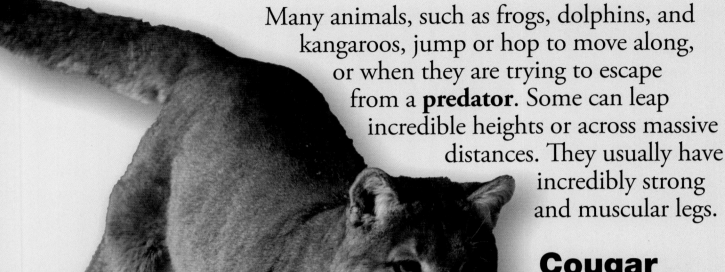

I am very quick and sure on my feet, like all big cats. I like following deer best, but often can't eat a whole deer all at once. I hide what's left and go back later to finish my meal.

Cougar

The cougar—also known as a puma or mountain lion—lives in many habitats in the Americas. It stalks and **ambushes** its **prey**, hiding in dense underbrush (plants, bushes, and trees). It can jump a long distance, both vertically and horizontally, which is useful to pounce on its prey.

Who else can jump high?

Kangaroo

This **marsupial**, like the wallaby, hops along on its strong back legs. It has long, elastic tendons in its hind legs to help it hop. The tail swings up and down when the kangaroo hops, balancing the body. A kangaroo hops up to four times its own length and at a speed of up to 50 mph (80 kph), but only over a short distance.

Flea

Fleas are the champion jumpers of the animal world. They need to be able to jump onto passing animals to feed. Tiny fleas can jump up to 12 in. (30 cm).

How do you take aim?

Some animals are natural archers, hitting their prey with incredible accuracy. Some use their whole bodies to launch themselves at and grab prey. Other animals use just a part of their bodies and take aim with that. The chameleon, for example, has a great weapon—its tongue! Some fish use water as a weapon and will shoot it out at passing targets.

Chameleon

This lizard's fused (joined) toes and strong tail help it hang tightly to branches while it concentrates on catching its prey. Chameleons hunt locusts, crickets, grasshoppers, and other insects. They move slowly through the trees until they get close enough to pounce. Some larger chameleons catch small birds and lizards.

I have a sticky tongue that is as long as my body. I shoot it out when I spot a tasty insect. When I am not using it to reel in prey, I pull it back into my throat out of the way.

Who else can aim?

Archerfish

This fish "shoots" insects off overhanging branches. It aims a jet of water at an insect up to 3 ft. (1 m) away, toppling the insect off of a perch and into the water, where it can be eaten. Archerfish learn to be accurate, and the adult fish almost always hit their target. The fish can even jump out of the water to catch their prey.

How do you glow in the dark?

In the darkest night or in the deepest parts of the oceans, there are some animals that have learned to survive by creating their own light. Some creatures release chemical energy, which helps them glow. Others release substances that light up.

Comb jelly

The comb jelly swims in the murky depths of many of the oceans. Its body is a mass of jelly and it swims through the water eating tiny animals called **zooplankton** that float there. Many comb jellies release chemical energy that causes them to glow with light.

I am **bioluminescent**—in other words, I can create light that helps to protect me from predators and also helps me find the creatures that I like to eat.

Who else can glow in the dark?

Firefly

The firefly is a beetle. The female's **abdomen** glows in order to attract a male for mating. Some fireflies glow to warn **predators**, such as frogs, that they are not good to eat.

Limpet

The freshwater limpet can make light in the dark, too. It makes a sticky goo that glows bright green and then lets the goo trail in the river current. The trail distracts hungry predators, such as eels.

Why do you play dead?

Some animals pretend they are dead in order to fool potential predators. The predator then thinks they are not worth investigating any further and moves away. The opossum is well-known for this trick and can play dead for several hours at a time.

Opossum

This ratlike **marsupial** is so well-known for this ability that playing dead is often described as "playing possum." Opossums live in trees and hunt at night. They play dead when they are cornered by predators and have no other way of escaping. They may lie in this position for up to six hours, and even let out a horrible smell to add to the effect.

> I am really good at playing dead—one of the best actors in the animal kingdom! I think the part where I let my mouth fall open is a nice touch, don't you? It fools most predators!

Who else plays dead?

Hognose snake

If a hognose snake cannot scare off another animal by flattening its neck and raising its head like a cobra, then it plays dead. It also lets out a horrible smell and lies on its back with its tongue hanging out of its mouth.

Lizard

There are several species of lizards that play dead when confronted by an attacker. They will lie on their back and stay very still, simply waiting until the animal that is a threat loses interest and goes away.

Who can see two things at once?

I can look all over the place to avoid danger or to find something tasty to eat. When I spot **prey**, my eyes work together to focus in on the target so that when I shoot out my sticky tongue, I will not miss!

Some creatures are very good at keeping an eye on things because they can look at two things at once! The chameleon is well-known for this and has eyes that can move in different directions!

Chameleon

The bulging eyes of the chameleon work independently from each other. The eyes can swivel in any direction, and this gives the lizard a useful 360-degree view around its body. Each eye has a scaly lid shaped like a cone. In the middle of each eye is a small, round opening for the pupil.

Who else sees two things at once?

Hammerhead shark

This shark has the most curious hammer-shaped head. Its eyes are placed at each end of the hammer shape. This means that it can see all around, but can also see what is above and below it at all times. This helps the shark maneuver easily in the water.

Sea horse

This fish is able to keep its eye on everything as it swims through the tropical waters. It also has eyes that move independently from each other. This helps it spot food or enemies.

Whose eyes are scariest?

Animals' eyes are often small and are not that scary, but some creatures have developed eyelike coloring or patterns that scare away **predators**. Many caterpillars, moths, and butterflies have patterns on their bodies or wings that look just like eyes, making them look like larger animals than they really are. Other animals can make their own eyes look bigger to make them look scarier.

> I don't need to worry much about large birds wanting to eat me. The eyespots on my head make any predator think that I am much larger than I actually am.

Spicebush caterpillar

The caterpillar of the spicebush swallowtail butterfly has very large false eyespots on its head. It also has a false mouth at the front of its head. It looks just like a snake to potential predators. Its real eyes and mouth are tucked in under the front of its head, well out of the way of any danger.

Who else has scary eyes?

Viper mimic

This caterpillar not only has a head and eyes shaped like a viper, but it has the same coloring and moves in the same way. It startles predators by inflating the front of its body to create this appearance, with its large eyes bulging out of its head.

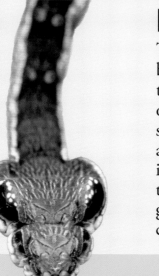

Buckeye moth

There are many butterflies and moths that have large eyespots on their wings to scare off birds. If a bird does attack, it will usually peck at the eyespots, and this gives the insect a chance to get away.

Why do you talk like that?

Animals need to communicate with one another, but they have a different way of "talking" than we do. Whales "sing" underwater to communicate with other whales, while gibbons hoot in the treetops. And some animals, such as the honeybee, "talk" and share important information without making a sound.

Humpback whale

The sounds that whales make underwater are called whale songs. The humpback whale, in particular, "sings" a pattern of regular sounds to communicate with their mates and their young. Sperm whales and dolphins, in contrast, do not sing, but make clicking sounds to talk to each other.

Who else can talk?

Gray wolf

Wolves communicate with growls, barks, and—most famous of all—howls. They growl at each other to communicate or growl to scare off other animals. They bark to raise the alarm, or sometimes to greet each other. The howls are usually used for long distance communication.

Golden hamster

This **rodent** has special scent glands on each hip. It uses these to scent mark its **territory**. The female also uses her scent glands to create an odor that communicates to a male that she is ready for mating.

Gibbon

Gibbons live in family groups and have an area that is their territory in the rainforest. Every morning for about 30 minutes, the group hoots to signal its presence and makes menacing gestures. This warns any other gibbon groups to stay away. Males and females have different calls.

I have the most beautiful song. I sing to attract a mate. My song can be heard over long distances, but the fin whale's song can be heard much farther away.

I really know how to make a noise! As I swing through the trees (and I am very good at that, too), I hoot loudly. I can be heard about ½ mi. (1 km) away.

What do we do?

When we are babies, we make gurgling and burbling sounds. We learn how to communicate with each other from our parents. We form words that other people around us will understand.

The figure eight dance

Honeybee

When a honeybee returns to the hives, it wants to tell the other bees about the amazing nectar it found. So it does a dance in a figure eight pattern. This gives the other bees the direction in which to travel to find the flowers and nectar. The honeybee has communicated to the others without making a single sound!

69

Why do you pretend to taste bad?

Animals that **mimic**, or copy, others do so to protect themselves. Some do this by behaving like others, but many do it by looking almost identical to the other animal and pretending to be poisonous to scare others away.

> I look almost the same as the monarch but I have a black line right across my bottom wings. But birds don't see such a small difference, and I normally get away because they are afraid of being poisoned.

Viceroy butterfly

Viceroy butterfly

The viceroy butterfly has developed to look almost the same as a monarch butterfly. This is because the monarch is poisonous to eat due to its milkweed diet. The viceroy fools its **predators** by making them think it is a monarch and not good to eat.

Monarch butterfly

Who else pretends to taste bad?

Wasp mimics

Wasps are very fierce insects and their sting can kill. So wasp mimics benefit greatly from the fact that they look very similar. Sometimes wasp mimics have the same long body as wasps, but the main similarity is the black and yellow warning stripes.

Wasp mimic

Wasp

How do you walk on water?

I manage to push the water down and away from my foot as I run. This creates a pocket of air around my foot and keeps me on the surface of the water for a distance of up to 15 ft. (4.5 m).

Water is not a barrier for some animals. Some creatures can move along its surface without any difficulty. The most amazing animal that does this is the basilisk lizard. It stays on the water's surface because of the shape of its feet and its extraordinary running style.

Basilisk lizard

When it is frightened by something, this lizard is able to run across the surface of the water to get away. The lizard runs on its hind legs for some distance and then sinks into the water and swims away.

Who else can walk on water?

Grebes

These waterbirds have a wonderful mating dance that they do in the spring. For part of this, they run side by side along the surface of the water. After a while, they dive down into the water together.

Fishing spider

These spiders live at the edges of ponds and streams. When insects drop into the water, the spiders run across the surface to attack. They can do this because of **surface tension** that makes the water surface behave like a thin, elastic film.

Can you laugh?

Some animals seem to enjoy laughing. But are they laughing or is it a different reaction to something in their **environment**? Chimpanzees seem to laugh like us, but other animals, such as hyenas, are actually howling rather than laughing.

I like to have a good laugh, particularly if I've been wrestling or tickling one of my brothers or sisters. We play chase a lot, too. That always makes me laugh.

Chimpanzee

There is no doubt that chimpanzees laugh as they play. These apes are very closely related to humans, so it is not surprising that they express their feelings in a similar way to us. They are social animals that respond to each other with a range of facial expressions.

Who else likes a good joke?

Hyena

A hyena makes a sound that is very close to hysterical laughter. It sort of howls. The animal opens its mouth in a way that makes it look like it is laughing. However, it normally makes this noise when it is anxious or fearful, or when it is competing for a small amount of food.

Kookaburra

The laughing kookaburra is so-named because it has a call that sounds like a laugh. But it is not really "laughing." Instead, it makes a low, hiccupping chuckle followed by a loud "laugh" when it or its family are establishing a **territory**.

Are you really electric?

Some fish can produce electricity. They do this to protect themselves from **predators**, to paralyze or kill their **prey**, or to find their way in waters where they cannot see clearly. In the case of the electric eel, the electricity that it generates helps it detect nearby objects.

> I have special muscles near the base of my pectoral fins that I use to produce the electricity. I am also sometimes called a numbfish, for obvious reasons!

What do we do?

All living creatures produce electricity. Electrons (ih-lek-TRONs) (particles with a charge of negative electricity) flow from one atom (particle) to another in our bodies. Our bodies are made up of atoms and so we are making electricity all the time.

Electric ray

This is a really electric fish that can stun prey or defend itself with a powerful electric shock. It is active during the day, lying well **camouflaged** on the seafloor. It is an **ambush** hunter, waiting until prey gets near enough to stun with an electric charge.

Who else is electric?

Knife fish

The nerve cells of this close relative of the electric eel produces a weak current, which it uses to sense its environment. It gets its name because it has a narrow body and a tapering tail, like a knife.

Electric eel

This fish produces strong electric currents when it is hunting. These currents stun its prey—other fish—with a shock. The fish then switches off the current and swallows the prey. It has special muscles down the length of its body, which act like batteries.

Are you really deadly?

There are some truly dangerous animals in the world, and many are poisonous. Some inject their poison, while others have poisonous skins. What they all have in common is that you are unlikely to see them before it is too late!

I am very poisonous indeed! If a snake or spider tries to pick me up, it gets a nasty surprise. I also have bright colors that say: "You won't want to eat me!"

Poison dart frog

Sometimes known as the poison arrow frog, this **amphibian** is famous because some South American tribes collect its poison and use it to make the tips of their darts deadly. Many of these frogs leak poisons through their skin, and this protects them from **predators**, such as snakes, which learn to avoid them.

Who else is deadly?
Cone shell

Some species of cone shells, marine snails, can fire a "barb" loaded with venom to subdue **prey**. The cone shell detects its prey using a siphon (SI-fun) (a tube-shaped organ), which senses where the prey is. It then shoots the poisonous spear through the siphon.

I only have to bite you once and you won't remember a thing. My venom is in my **saliva**. It is stronger than most poisons found on land, and it paralyzes my victims.

Blue-ringed octopus

This tiny octopus has the most deadly bite of them all. It is very beautiful but it can kill a human in less than 15 minutes with its poisonous bite. It lives off the coast of Australia and is named after the bright blue rings that cover its body.

Stonefish

The stonefish is so-named because of its stonelike appearance. It sits on the seabed and waits for its unsuspecting prey to swim by. The **spines** in its dorsal fin are poisonous and can be deadly to humans who step on them accidentally.

King cobra

The king cobra is the longest venomous snake in the world. One strike from this snake is enough to bring down an elephant. The cobra is able to rear up with a third of its body off the ground and attack. It delivers enough poison to kill 20 people in a single deadly bite.

Glossary

abdomen
The back part of an insect's body. The abdomen is made up of six or more jointed parts.

ambush
To lie hidden in wait in order to attack an animal by surprise.

amphibian
An animal that begins life in water but can live on land when it is an adult.

barbel
A thick "hair" that sticks out from the mouth of some fish—it looks like a cat's whisker. The fish uses its barbels to find food in the mud.

bioluminescent
When an animal produces light to communicate or help it see.

black smoker
A chimneylike opening on the floor of the sea from which hot, mineral-rich liquid from the Earth's mantle flows.

camouflage
A color pattern or body shape that helps hide an animal in its surroundings.

contract
To draw parts of the body together to become smaller.

environment
The external surroundings in which an animal lives.

estivate
To sleep through a hot, dry season.

herbivore
An animal that eats only plants.

hibernate
To sleep deeply through the winter.

krill
Small, shrimplike animals that float in the oceans.

larva (plural: larvae)
The second stage in the life of an insect, between the egg and the adult stages.

mammal
An animal that gives birth to live young that feed on their mother's milk.

mangrove
A tree that grows in shallow coastal water in hot parts of the world.

marsupial
An animal that has a pouch on the outside of its body. The young of the animal develop inside the pouch.

microscopic
Something that is so small that it cannot be seen by our eyes alone.

migrate
To move from one place to another. Animals migrate to find food, produce young, or to escape from cold weather.

mimic
To look like, or behave like, another animal. Some insects mimic others that bite, or are poisonous, in order to protect themselves from attacks.

navigate
To find the way from one place to another.

nocturnal
Describes an animal that is active at night.

nutrient
The part of food that can be used by an animal for health and growth.

photophore
A glowing organ found in certain fish and crustaceans.

plankton
The tiny plants and animals that float near the surface of the seas, oceans, and rivers.

predator
An animal that hunts and eats other animals.

prey
An animal that is hunted and eaten by other animals.

pride
A group of lions.

reptile
An animal that has dry, scaly skin and usually lays eggs. Reptiles cannot make their own body heat.

rodent
An animal that has long front teeth that it uses for gnawing.

saliva
A watery fluid in the mouth that helps animals taste, chew, and swallow food.

spiderling
A baby spider.

spine
One of the needlelike parts that cover the outside of some animals. Porcupines and puffer fish have spines.

surface tension
The elasticlike skin on the surface of water that stops some insects and animals from sinking into the water.

syrinx
The vocal organ of birds.

talon
One of the sharp, hooked claws on the foot of a hunting bird.

tentacle
A long arm, or feeler, of some animals, used for feeling, moving, holding, or stinging.

territory
The area of land lived in and guarded by a bird or animal.

zooplankton
Plankton that consists of tiny animals.

Index

Acknowledgments

Marshall Editions would like to thank the following agencies for supplying images for inclusion in this book:

Key: t = top, c = center, b = bottom, l = left, r = right

Inside: 1 Shutterstock/Eric Isselée; 3 Shutterstock/Christian Musat; 5cl Shutterstock/orionmystery@flickr; 5cr Shutterstock/Eric Isselée; 5bl Shutterstock/Ivaschenko Roman; 5br Shutterstock/Eric Isselée; 6cl Shutterstock/Eric Isselée; 6bl Shutterstock/Eric Isselée; 6bc Nature PL/Brandon Cole; 6br Shutterstock/Chen Wei Seng; 6/7t Shutterstock/Mark Dumbleton; 6/7cl Shutterstock/Arto Hakola; 6/7cr Nature PL/Edwin Giesbers; 7tc NHPA/Daniel Deuclin; 7tr Alamy/Chris Mattison; 7cr Shutterstock/Leighton Photography & Imaging; 7cr Nature PL/Jane Eurton; 7bl Shutterstock/Sam D Cruz; 7bc Shutterstock/Mike Truchon; 7br Shutterstock/Alex James Bramwell; 8l Shutterstock/Five Spots; 8/9 Shutterstock/Tarasov; 9tc Shutterstock/Chad Littlejohn; 9r Shutterstock/Alex James Bramwell; 9b Shutterstock/Four Oaks; 10t Shutterstock/Alex James Bramwell; 10bl Shutterstock/Ng Wei Keong; 10br Nature PL/Stephen Dalton; 11tr Shutterstock/Michael G. Mill; 11bl Photolibrary/Ariadne Van Zandbergen; 12bl Photolibrary/Morales Morales; 12/13 Photolibrary/L Peck Michael; 13tr Nature PL/Tony Heald; 13bl Photolibrary/Mark Hamblin; 13br Photolibrary/Ronald Wittek; 14t Photolibrary/James H Robinson; 14bl Shutterstock/Jiri Foltyn; 14br Shutterstock/Eric Isselée; 15tl Shutterstock/Eric Isselée; 15tr Shutterstock/Dr. Morley Read; 15bl Shutterstock/Michael Lynch; 15br Shutterstock/Four Oaks; 16t Shutterstock/Tarasov; 16bl Shutterstock/Mashe; 16br Shutterstock/Rey Kamensky; 17tr Shutterstock/Five Spots; 17bl Corbis/Stephen Frink; 17br Corbis/Steven Kazlowski; 18tl Nature PL/Mark Carwadine; 18bl Shutterstock/Eric Isselée; 18br Shutterstock/Debr22pics; 19tr Nature PL/Dave Bevan; 19bl Ardea/Francois Gohier; 19br Shutterstock/Eric Isselée; 20tr Nature PL/Jane Eurton; 20bl Nature PL/John Cancalosi; 20br Getty Images/Don Farrall; 21tr NHPA/Martin Harvey; 21bl Getty Images/Paul Souders; 21br NHPA/Daniel Deuclin; 22t Shutterstock/Chad Littlejohn; 22bl Shutterstock/Matyas Arvai; 22br Nature PL/Philippe Clement; 23tr Shutterstock/Eric Isselée; 23bl Shutterstock/Eric Isselée; 23br Photolibrary/Randy Morse;

24t FLPA/Image Broker; 24bl Corbis; 24/25b Corbis/Paul A. Souders; 25t FLPA/Jurgen & Christine Sohns; 25br Nature PL/Edwin Giesbers; 26tl Shutterstock/Christian Musat; 26bl Shutterstock/Pix2go; 26br Nature PL/Brandon Cole; 27tr Shutterstock/Eric Isselée; 27bl Shutterstock/Mike Price; 27br Shutterstock/Five Spots; 28cl Shutterstock/Tischenko Irina; 28/29t Shutterstock/Kirsanov; 28/29b Shutterstock/Vitaly Korovin; 29tr Shutterstock/Ishbukar Yalilfatar; 28/29 Shutterstock/Mark Dumbleton; 30t Shutterstock/Florida Stock; 30bl Nature PL/Reinhard/Arco; 30br Shutterstock/Jim Nelson; 31t Shutterstock/Kirsanov; 31bl Shutterstock/Audrey Snider-Bell; 31br Nature PL/David Shale; 32tl Shutterstock/Stefan Schejok; 32bl Photolibrary/Paul Kay; 32br Photolibrary/Karen Gowlett-Holmes; 33t Shutterstock/Irina Tischenko; 33bl Shutterstock/Eric Isselée; 33br Shutterstock/Attl Tibor; 34tl Shutterstock/Inginsh; 34bl Shutterstock/Eric Isselée; 34/35 Shutterstock/Melinda Fawer; 35tr Shutterstock/Kirsanov; 35br Shutterstock/Vitaly Korovin; 36t Shutterstock/Ishbukar Yalilfatar; 36bl Shutterstock/Armin Rose; 36br Shutterstock/Prochasson Frederic; 37t Shutterstock/Airn; 37bl Nature PL/Constantinos Petrinos; 37br Photolibrary/Michael Habicht; 38tl Shutterstock/David W Hughes; 38bl Shutterstock/Coprid; 38br Shutterstock; 39tr Shutterstock/Mark Dumbleton; 39bl Shutterstock/Eric Isselée; 39br Shutterstock/Roman Ivaschenko; 40tr Shutterstock/Eric Isselée; 40bl Shutterstock/Eric Isselée; 40-41b Corbis/Daniel J. Cox; 41tl Shutterstock/Eric Isselée; 41r Shutterstock/Rey Kamensky; 42t Nature PL/David Shale; 42bl Nature PL/David Shale; 42-43b Photolibrary/Thomas Haider; 43tr Nature PL/David Shale; 43br Nature PL/Doc White; 44t Corbis/Daniel J. Cox; 44bl Getty Images/AFP; 45t Shutterstock/Eric Isselée; 45bl Nature PL/Ingo Arndt; 45br Shutterstock/Sebastian Knight; 46t Shutterstock/Eric Isselée; 46bl Shutterstock/Johan Swanepoel; 46br Nature PL/Jeff Rotman; 47t Shutterstock/Five Spots; 47bl NOAA; 47br Photolibrary/Robert Maier; 48t Nature PL/Chris Gomersall; 48bl Shutterstock/Fotique; 48br Photolibrary/Joerg Reuther; 49t Shutterstock/Eric Isselée; 49bl Corbis/Peter Johnson; 49br Shutterstock/Argonaut; 50tl Shutterstock/Eric Isselée; 50bl Photolibrary/John Pitcher; 50/51b Photolibrary/Stouffer Productions; 51tr

Shutterstock/Eric Isselée; 51br Photolibrary/Owen Newman; 52t Shutterstock/Eric Isselée; 52bl Photolibrary/Jonathan Bird; 52br Corbis/Mike Jones; 53t Nature PL/Neil Bromhall; 53bl Photolibrary/Paul Freed; 53br Photolibrary/Max Gibbs; 54t Shutterstock/Eric Isselée; 54bl Shutterstock/Four Oaks; 54br Shutterstock/Lucas Photos; 55bl Photolibrary/Superstock Inc; 55r Shutterstock/Rey Kamensky; 56cl Shutterstock/Igor Karon; 56br Shutterstock/Nicola Vernizzi; 56/57t Nature PL/Juan Carlos Munoz; 57tr Shutterstock/Le Do; 57cr Shutterstock/Cathy Keifer; 57b Nature PL/Doug Wechsler; 58tl Shutterstock/Lidara; 58bl Getty Images/Norbert Wu; 59cl Alamy/Chris Mattison; 59l Shutterstock/orionmystery@flickr; 59bl Shutterstock/Andy Lidstone; 60t Shutterstock/Mike Truchon; 60bl Shutterstock/Irin-k; 60br Nature PL/Stephen Dalton; 61t Nature PL/Ingo Arndt; 61bl Shutterstock/Five Spots; 61br Photolibrary/Juniors Bildarchiv; 62t Shutterstock/Dennis Donohue; 62bl Photolibrary/Joerg Hauke; 62br Nature PL/Stephen Dalton; 63tr Nature PL/Stephen Dalton; 63br Nature PL/Kim Taylor; 64t Nature PL/David Fleetham; 64bl Shutterstock/Cathy Keifer; 64br Nature PL/Wild Wonders of Europe/Lundgren; 65t Shutterstock/Stacy Barnett; 65bl Corbis/Jim Merli; 65br Alamy/O. D. Vande Deer; 66tl Shutterstock/Cathy Keifer; 66bl Nature PL/Brandon Cole; 66br Shutterstock/Chen Wei Seng; 67t Nature PL/Doug Wechsler; 67bl Alamy/Photoshot Holdings Ltd; 67br Shutterstock/Leighton Photography & Imaging; 68t Nature PL/Brandon Cole; 68bl Shutterstock/Eric Isselée; 68br Shutterstock; 69tr Nature PL/Juan Carlos Munoz; 69bl Shutterstock/Peter Waters; 70tl Shutterstock/Le Do; 70tr Shutterstock/Cathy Keifer; 70bl Shutterstock/Melinda Fawver; 70br Shutterstock/Arto Hakola; 71t Nature PL/Bence Mate; 71bl Photolibrary/Barbara Von Hoffman; 71br Alamy/Blickwinkel; 72t Shutterstock/Igor Karon; 72bl Nature PL/Hermann Brehm; 72br Shutterstock/Andrew Chin; 73t Nature PL/Peter Scoones; 73bl Corbis/Jerry Young; 73br Photolibrary/Zigmund Leszozynski; 74tr Shutterstock/Nicola Vernizzi; 74bl Science Photo Library/Dr George Gornacz; 74br Shutterstock/Stephan Kerkhofs; 75t Shutterstock/ Teguh Tirtaputra; 75b Shutterstock/Sam DCruz 77br Shutterstock/Dennis Donohue.